Is it a living thing?

Bobbie Kalman

🌳 **Crabtree Publishing Company**

www.crabtreebooks.com

Created by Bobbie Kalman

To Phyllis, who has been my friend since we were teens,
with much love from Babi

**Author and
Editor-in-Chief**
Bobbie Kalman

Editors
Reagan Miller
Robin Johnson

Photo research
Crystal Sikkens

Design
Bobbie Kalman
Katherine Kantor
Samantha Crabtree (cover)

Production coordinator
Katherine Kantor

Illustrations
Barbara Bedell: pages 6, 12 (bottom), 22, 23, 24 (cells, rain forest, reptile,
    and newt life cycle)
Antoinette "Cookie" Bortolon: pages 12 (top), 24 (girl)
Katherine Kantor: pages 16, 17, 24 (fish and skeleton)

Photographs
© iStockphoto.com: front cover, 5 (top left), 13 (bottom), 14 (top flower)
© 2008 Jupiterimages Corporation: pages 11 (top), 20, 21 (bottom)
© ShutterStock.com: back cover, pages 1, 3, 4, 5 (top right and bottom),
    7, 8, 9, 10, 11 (bottom and background), 12, 13 (top), 14 (bottom flowers),
    15 (bottom flowers), 16, 17, 18, 19, 21 (top), 22, 24
Other images by Corbis and Digital Stock

Library and Archives Canada Cataloguing in Publication

Kalman, Bobbie, 1947-
    Is it a living thing? / Bobbie Kalman.

(Introducing living things)
Includes index.
ISBN 978-0-7787-3230-3 (bound).--ISBN 978-0-7787-3254-9 (pbk.)

    1. Life (Biology)--Juvenile literature. I. Title. II. Series.

QH309.2.K24 2007   j570   C2007-904672-X

Library of Congress Cataloging-in-Publication Data

Kalman, Bobbie.
    Is it a living thing? / Bobbie Kalman.
        p. cm. -- (Introducing living things)
    Includes index.
    ISBN-13: 978-0-7787-3230-3 (rlb)
    ISBN-10: 0-7787-3230-4 (rlb)
    ISBN-13: 978-0-7787-3254-9 (pb)
    ISBN-10: 0-7787-3254-1 (pb)
    1. Life (Biology)--Juvenile literature. I. Title. II. Series.

QH309.2.K23 2008
570--dc22

2007029996

Crabtree Publishing Company

www.crabtreebooks.com   1-800-387-7650

Published in Canada
Crabtree Publishing
616 Welland Ave.
St. Catharines, Ontario
L2M 5V6

Published in the United States
Crabtree Publishing
PMB16A
350 Fifth Ave., Suite 3308
New York, NY 10118

Published in the United Kingdom
Crabtree Publishing
White Cross Mills
High Town, Lancaster
LA1 4XS

Published in Australia
Crabtree Publishing
386 Mt. Alexander Rd.
Ascot Vale (Melbourne)
VIC 3032

Contents

Is it a living thing?

What is a **living thing**? Plants are living things. Animals are living things. People are living things. Living things grow and change. They move. These dolphins are leaping out of water. Are dolphins plants or animals?

Living things need air, water, and food. Most living things also need sunshine. Name all the living things you see on these pages.

Tiny cells

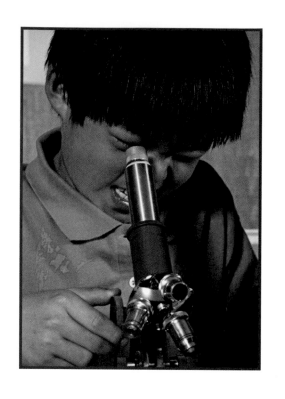

All living things are made of **cells**. A cell is tiny. You can see it only with a **microscope**. Some living things are made of just one kind of cell. Other living things have many kinds of cells. Animals and people have many kinds of cells.

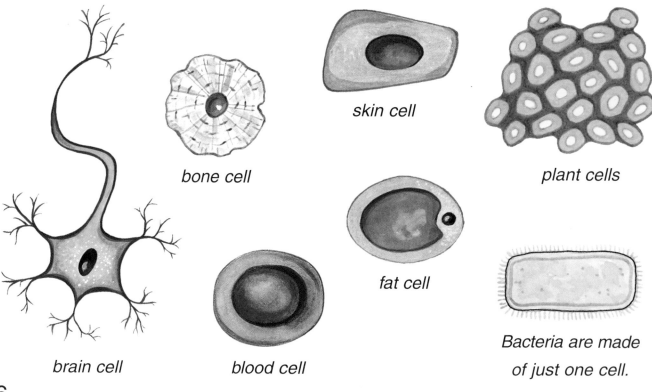

bone cell

skin cell

plant cells

fat cell

brain cell

blood cell

Bacteria are made of just one cell.

6

How do cells look under a microscope? Some cells are shown on this page. These green cells are called **chlorophyll**. They are part of plants. They give plants their color.

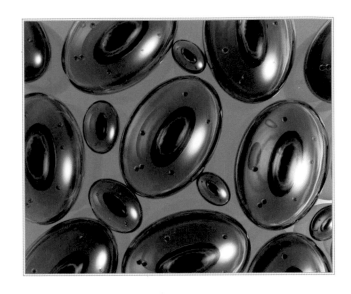

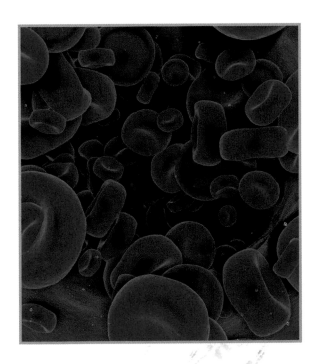

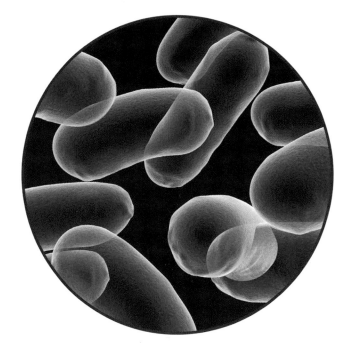

These red cells are blood cells. You have millions of blood cells in your body.

These are bacteria cells. Some kinds of bacteria can make people sick.

Non-living things

Air, water, sunshine, soil, and rocks are **non-living things**. These things are not made of cells. Non-living things are very important to living things. Living things could not stay alive without them.

Sea stars live among rocks in oceans. Sea stars are living things. Rocks are non-living things.

Plants need air, water, and sunshine to grow. Many plants grow in soil. Their roots find water under the ground. Some plants grow in soil that is under water.

Sunshine is energy

Living things need **energy**. Living things cannot do anything without it. Living things need energy to move and to grow. All energy comes from the sun. Plants take in the sun's energy and use it to make food. Plants are the only living things that can make food from sunshine.

The energy of the sun is in plants. When animals eat plants, they get the energy of the sun, too. When energy is passed from one living thing to another, there is a **food chain**.

The sun's energy is in this flower. When the groundhog eats the flower, it will also get the sun's energy. The sun, the flower, and the groundhog make up a food chain.

Animals and people need sunshine to keep their bodies warm. These turtles have come out of the water to warm their bodies in the sun.

Air and water

Plants need air to make food. They use a part of air called **carbon dioxide**. They breathe out **oxygen**. Animals and people need to breathe oxygen. How do plants and animals breathe? These pictures will show you.

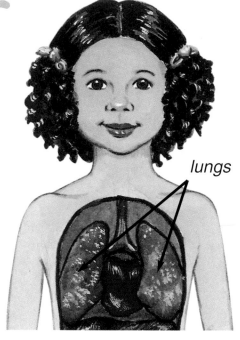

lungs

People and many animals breathe using **lungs**.

Fish breathe using **gills**.

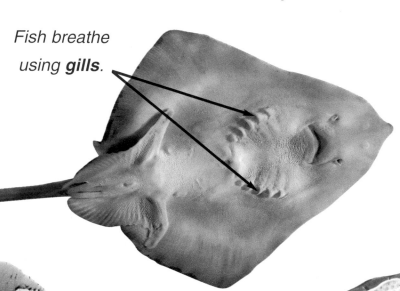

Frogs breathe through their skin as well as with lungs.

Insects breathe through **small** holes called **spiracles**.

Plants breathe through tiny holes called **stomata**.

All living things need water, too. Plants need water to make food. Animals need to drink water. Our bodies are made mostly of water. We need to drink water to keep our bodies healthy. Many animals live in water. These fish live in an ocean.

Kinds of plants

Flowers, trees, bushes, and weeds are plants. Most plants have roots, leaves, and stems. Some plants have fruits. What kind of plants are these?

flower

stem

leaves

roots

tree

bush

Trees are the biggest plants. They can grow in soil or in water. Bushes are smaller than trees. Weeds grow almost everywhere. There are some weeds among the flowers below.

15

Animal bones

All animals are living things. Animals that have **backbones** inside their bodies are called **vertebrates**. There are five kinds of vertebrates. They are fish, birds, **reptiles**, **amphibians**, and **mammals**.

This is a fish's backbone. Fish are vertebrates.

This chameleon is a reptile.
Reptiles are vertebrates.

This owl is a bird.
Birds are vertebrates.

Frogs belong to a group of animals called
amphibians. Amphibians are vertebrates.

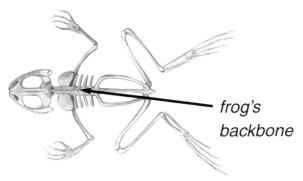

frog's
backbone

Dogs and people are mammals.
Mammals are vertebrates.

17

No backbones

Animals can be very small. Animals can be very big. Some animals have backbones inside their bodies. Most of the animals on Earth have no backbones. Animals that have no backbones inside their bodies are called **invertebrates**. Insects are invertebrates. This insect is a grasshopper.

Spiders, moths, and worms are some invertebrates that live on land.

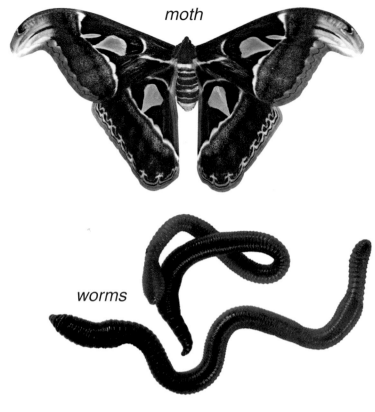

moth

spider

worms

Many invertebrates live in oceans. Crabs and sea stars are invertebrates that live in oceans.

sea star

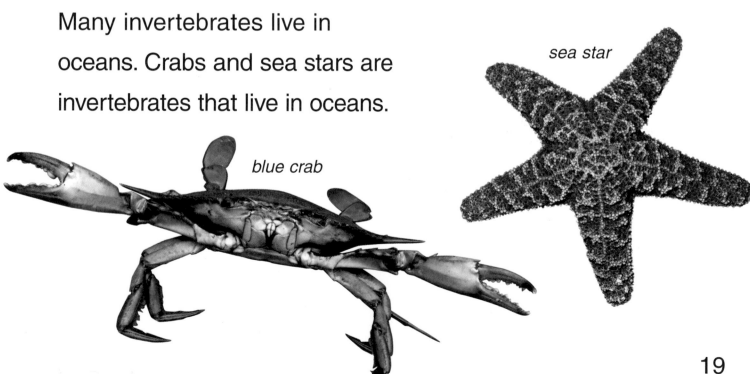

blue crab

Where do they live?

Living things need places to live. Living things find water and food where they live. Plants grow almost everywhere. They can grow in cold places and in hot places. These plants are growing in a **rain forest**. Rain forests get a lot of rain. Many kinds of animals, like this toucan, live in rain forests.

These young mountain goats live high up in a mountain habitat. Do not look down!

Different plants and animals live in different **habitats**. A habitat is the natural place where a plant or an animal lives. Mountains and deserts are some habitats. Oceans, lakes, and ponds are other habitats. People live indoors in homes that are built.

These kit foxes live in deserts in the United States and in Mexico.

21

Grow and change

bean plant

Living things grow and change. Plants grow and make new plants. This bean plant is making seeds that will grow into new bean plants. Animals grow and become **adults**. Adult animals can make babies. People also have babies. Human babies are **born**. Many animal babies are born, too. Some animals **hatch** from eggs.

Baby birds hatch from eggs.
This baby bird has just hatched.

A newt's life cycle

Every living thing has a **life cycle**. A life cycle is all the changes a living thing goes through from the time it is a baby to the time it is an adult. Some animals change a lot. This newt started its life in water as a **tadpole**. The newt is now an adult and can live on land.

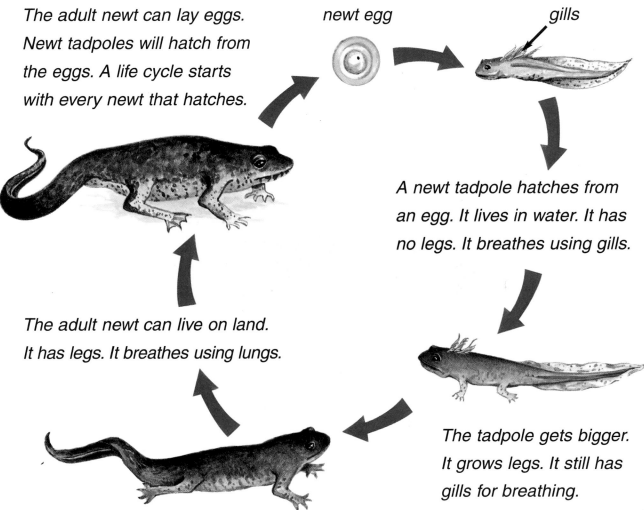

The adult newt can lay eggs. Newt tadpoles will hatch from the eggs. A life cycle starts with every newt that hatches.

newt egg

gills

A newt tadpole hatches from an egg. It lives in water. It has no legs. It breathes using gills.

The adult newt can live on land. It has legs. It breathes using lungs.

The tadpole gets bigger. It grows legs. It still has gills for breathing.

23

Words to know and Index

amphibians
pages 16, 17

hatch

birds
pages 16, 17, 22

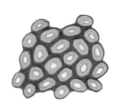

cells
pages 6-7, 8

fish
pages 12, 13, 16

rain forest

habitats
page 21

spider

invertebrates
pages 18-19

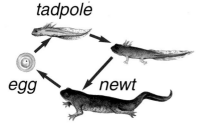
tadpole *egg* *newt*

life cycle
page 23

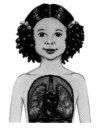

lungs
pages 12, 23

mammals
pages 16, 17

soil

plants
pages 4, 6, 7, 9, 10, 11, 12, 13, 14-15, 20, 21, 22

reptiles
pages 16, 17

skeleton *backbone*

vertebrates
pages 16-17

Other index words

air pages 5, 8, 9, 12

breathing pages 12, 23

energy pages 10, 11

non-living things page 8

sunshine pages 5, 8, 9, 10, 11

water pages 4, 5, 8, 9, 11, 12, 13, 15, 20, 23

24